Cranes

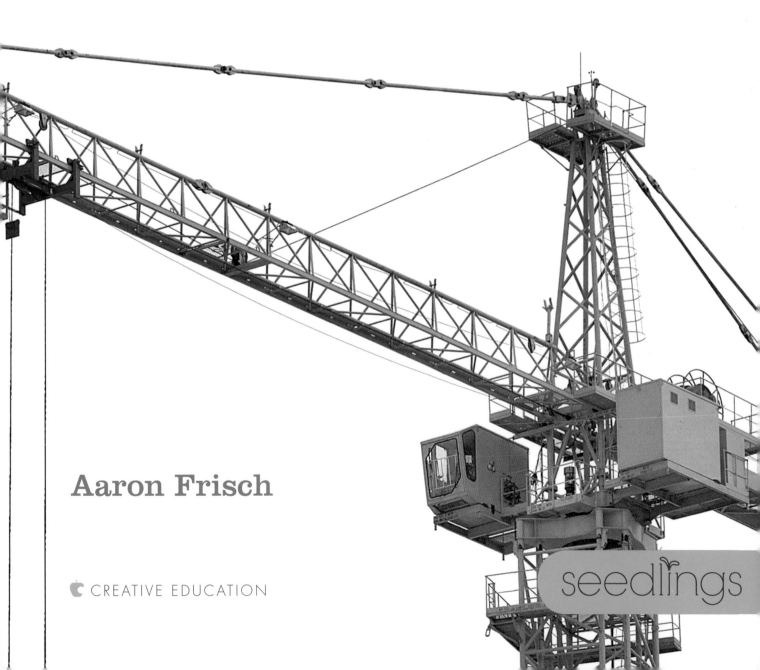

Aaron Frisch

CREATIVE EDUCATION

seedlings

Published by Creative Education
P.O. Box 227, Mankato, Minnesota 56002
Creative Education is an imprint of
The Creative Company
www.thecreativecompany.us

Design by Ellen Huber
Production by Chelsey Luther
Art direction by Rita Marshall
Printed in the United States of America

Photographs by Corbis (Alan Schein Photography),
Dreamstime (Alisonh29, Simas Bernotas, Photoarts30,
Alexander Potapov, Youths), iStockphoto (choicegraphx),
Shutterstock (corepics, Faraways, Paula Fisher, vita
khorzhevska, Philip Lange, Tonis Pan, Vakhrushev Pavel,
Potapov Alexander, pryzmat, SSSCCC, James Steidl, Edwin
Verin, kao wenhua)

Library of Congress Cataloging-in-Publication Data
Frisch, Aaron.
Cranes / Aaron Frisch.
p. cm. — (Seedlings)
Summary: A kindergarten-level introduction to cranes,
covering their size, movement, role in the process of
construction, and such defining features as their arms
and cables.
Includes bibliographical references and index.
ISBN 978-1-60818-339-5
1. Cranes, derricks, etc.—Juvenile literature. I. Title.

TJ1363.F75 2013
621.8'73—dc23   2012023308

First Edition
9 8 7 6 5 4 3 2 1

TABLE OF CONTENTS

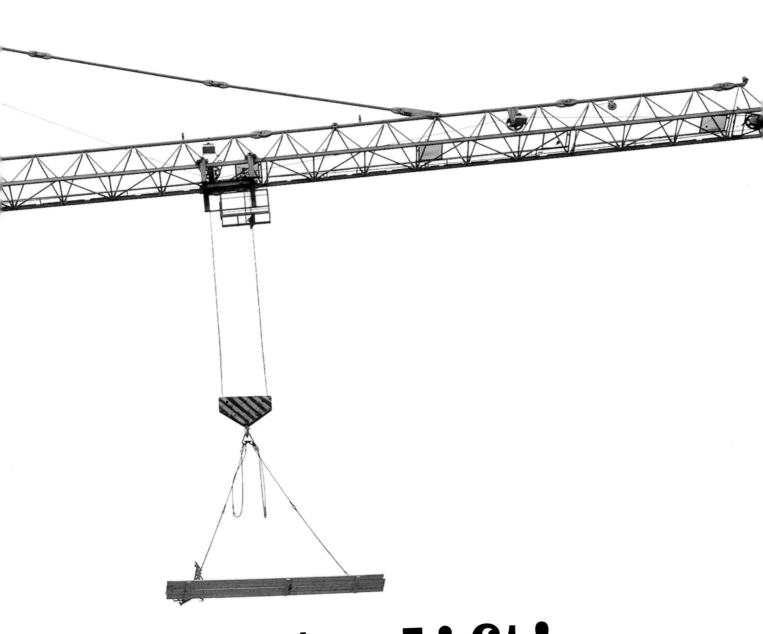

Time to lift!

Cranes are tall machines. They lift metal parts. They move big boxes around.

A crane has a long arm.

Strong cables hang down from the arm.

There is a bucket
or hook on the
end of the cable.

It lets a crane pick things up.

The bottom part of a crane does not move. Only the arm and cables move.

Cranes can be big or small. Some cranes swing a wrecking ball to knock down buildings.

Cranes help
build skyscrapers.
They put things
on ships.

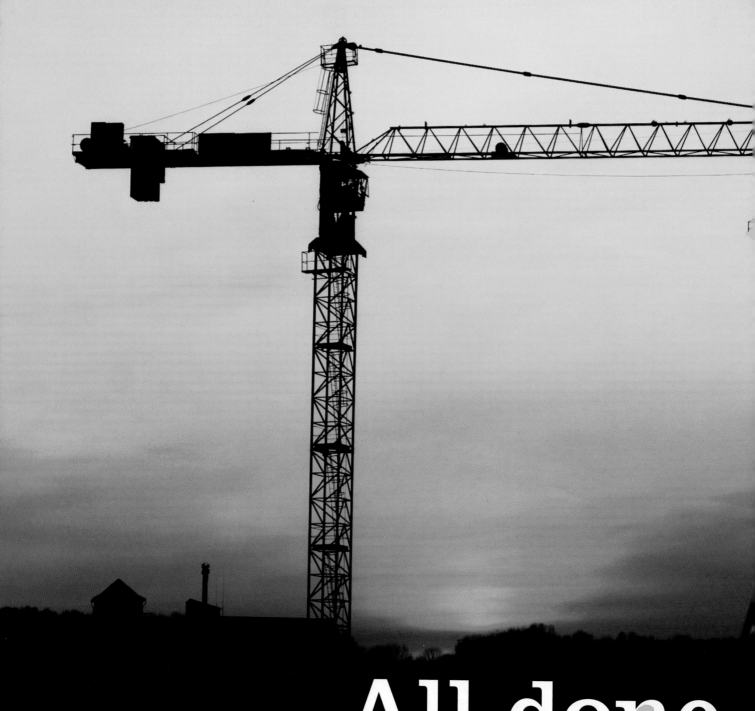

All done

lifting!

Picture a Crane

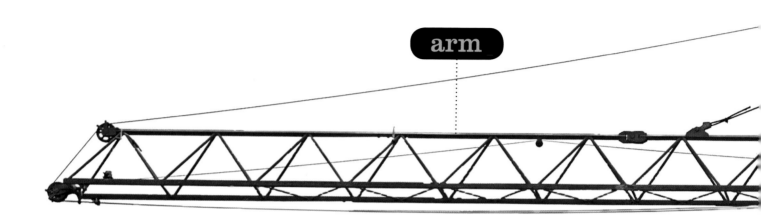

arm

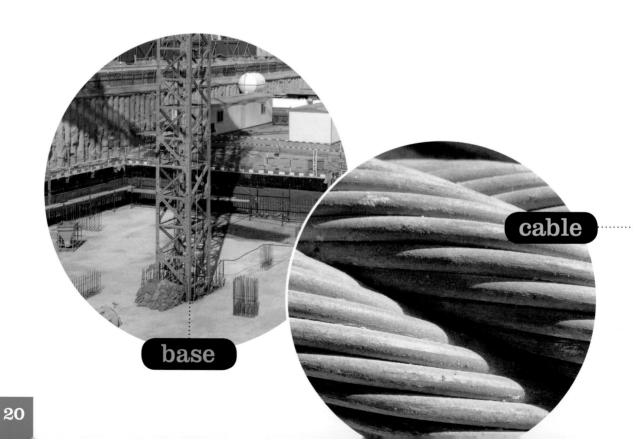

base

cable

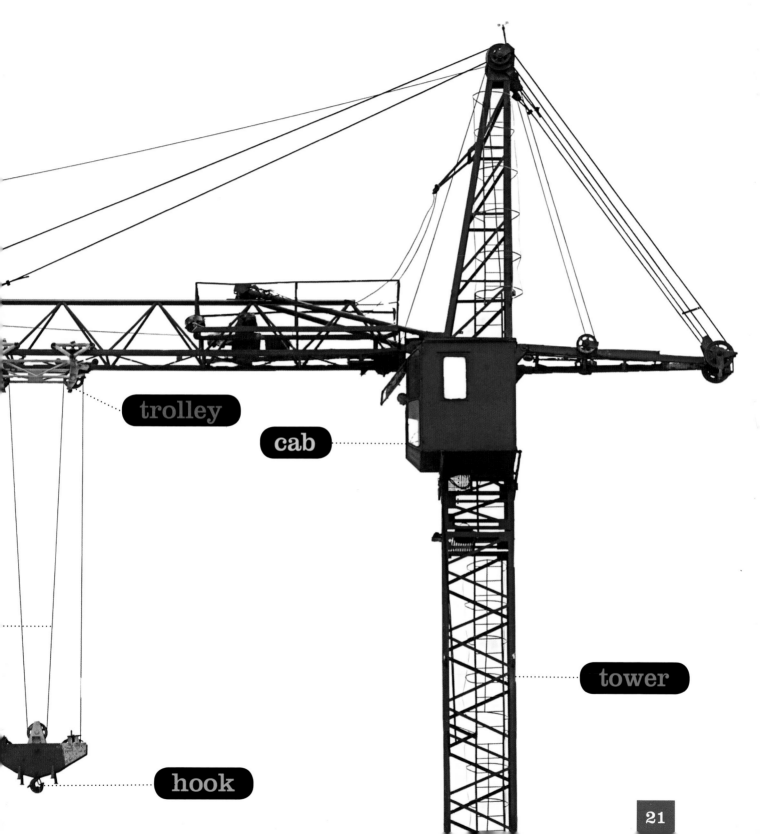

trolley

cab

tower

hook

21

Words to Know

arm: a long part that can reach and move

cables: strong cords that are like metal ropes

skyscrapers: very tall buildings

wrecking ball: a big, heavy ball used to smash things

Read More

Martin, M. T. *Cranes*.
Minneapolis: Bellwether, 2007.

Sobel, June. *B Is for Bulldozer: A Construction ABC*.
San Diego: Gulliver Books, 2003.

Websites

Crawler Construction Crane
http://www.looledo.com/index.php/crawler-construction-crane.html
This site tells you how to build your own crane.

Free Construction Coloring Pages
http://www.squidoo.com/free-construction-coloring-pages
This site has crane pictures. You can print and color them.

Index

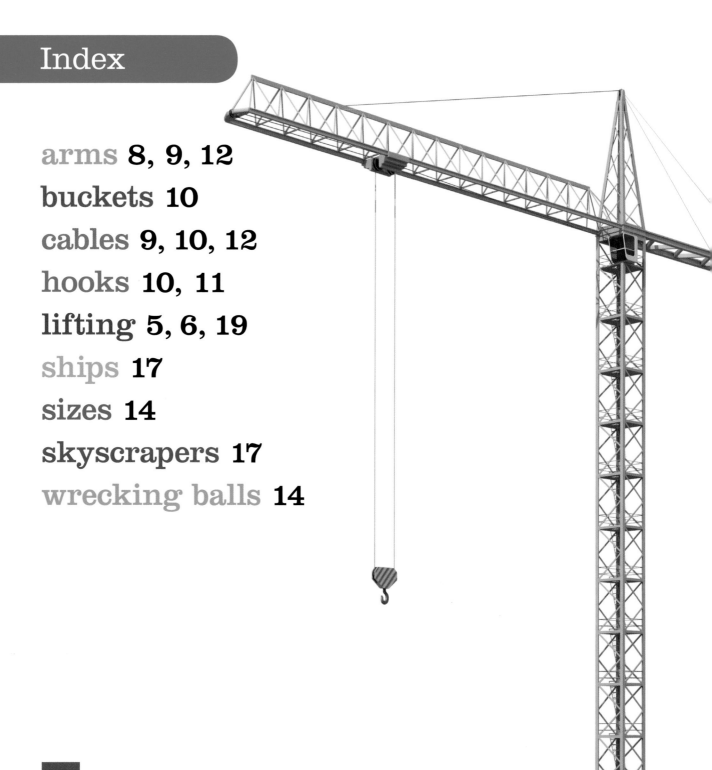